Against the Tide: Survival Stories from the Tsunami's Wake

ANTOINETTE KLEINHANS

Table Of Contents

Chapter 1: The Calm Before the Storm — 2

Chapter 2: The Day of Destruction — 6

Chapter 3: Survival Instincts — 11

Chapter 4: Finding Shelter — 17

Chapter 5: The Aftermath — 22

Chapter 6: Rebuilding Lives — 27

Chapter 7: Lessons Learned — 32

Chapter 8: Inspiring Hope — 37

Chapter 9: A Call to Action — 42

Chapter 10: Reflections on Survival — 48

Chapter 1: The Calm Before the Storm

The Signs We Ignored

In the aftermath of the tsunami, many survivors reflected on the signs they had overlooked in the days leading up to the disaster. These signs, often dismissed as mere anomalies or coincidences, served as subtle warnings of the impending catastrophe. The rumbling of the earth, unusual animal behavior, and sudden changes in ocean currents were all indicators that something was amiss. By examining these overlooked cues, we gain insight into the importance of vigilance and preparedness in the face of nature's unpredictability.

The first sign that many ignored was the earth's tremors. In the days preceding the tsunami, residents felt an increase in seismic activity. While earthquakes are common in many regions, the frequency and intensity of these tremors were unusual. Some dismissed them as routine geological movements, failing to connect the dots between the quakes and the potential for a larger disaster. This highlights the critical need for communities to educate themselves about natural signs and to take them seriously, recognizing that sometimes what seems ordinary can foreshadow extraordinary events.

Animal behavior also provided a significant, yet often overlooked, warning. Reports emerged of animals fleeing to higher ground long before the tsunami struck. Pets became restless, and wildlife altered their usual patterns, sensing impending danger. Many people, however, attributed this behavior to other causes, such as changes in weather or food availability. This serves as a poignant reminder that nature communicates in ways we may not fully understand, and it encourages us to pay attention to the world around us. By fostering a deeper connection with nature, we can learn to read these signs more effectively.

The sudden shifts in ocean currents, too, went largely unnoticed. In coastal areas, residents observed receding waters that left beaches exposed in ways they had never seen before. This phenomenon, a precursor to a tsunami, was misinterpreted by many as a mere ebb tide. Understanding these oceanic signs is crucial, as they signal a looming danger. Educating communities about these indicators can empower individuals to act swiftly and seek safety, potentially saving lives in moments of crisis.

In retrospect, the signs that were ignored serve as valuable lessons for future preparedness. They urge us to cultivate a mindset of awareness and readiness in the face of natural disasters. By documenting and sharing these experiences, we can create a culture that prioritizes vigilance and encourages proactive measures. Ultimately, recognizing the signs of nature can enhance our resilience and ability to survive, transforming our approach to disaster preparedness and response in a world where unpredictability is the only constant.

Life in Coastal Communities

Life in coastal communities is often characterized by a unique blend of beauty and vulnerability. The picturesque views of endless horizons and the rhythmic sounds of waves crashing against the shore create a serene backdrop for daily life. Residents of these areas cultivate a deep connection to the ocean, shaping their culture, economy, and social structures around marine resources. Fishing, tourism, and maritime activities are not only sources of livelihood but also integral to the identity of these communities. However, this close relationship with the sea comes with inherent risks, especially as climate change and natural disasters pose increasing threats to their existence.

In the aftermath of a tsunami, the resilience of coastal communities is put to the test. The immediate devastation is often overwhelming, with homes, infrastructure, and livelihoods obliterated. Yet, amid the chaos, the spirit of community emerges as a powerful force for recovery. Neighbors come together to support one another, sharing resources, information, and emotional strength. This solidarity plays a crucial role in rebuilding efforts, as residents work collectively to restore their homes and lives. The shared experience of loss fosters a sense of camaraderie that transcends individual grief, allowing communities to heal and move forward.

Rebuilding after a disaster is not solely about physical structures; it also involves revitalizing the social and economic fabric of coastal life. Many communities adopt innovative approaches to reconstruction, incorporating sustainable practices that reduce future risks. This may include creating buffer zones with natural barriers like mangroves or implementing advanced early warning systems. By embracing resilience as a guiding principle, these communities not only recover but also enhance their ability to withstand future challenges. The lessons learned from the tsunami serve as a catalyst for change, encouraging proactive measures that prioritize safety and sustainability.

Education plays a pivotal role in shaping the future of coastal communities. Engaging local populations in disaster preparedness and response training empowers them to take charge of their safety and well-being. Schools and community centers often become hubs for sharing knowledge about emergency protocols, environmental stewardship, and resource management. Children grow up understanding the importance of resilience and the necessity of respecting the ocean's power. This cultural shift towards preparedness and adaptability ensures that future generations are better equipped to navigate the complexities of living in harmony with nature.

Ultimately, life in coastal communities is a testament to the human spirit's capacity for resilience and renewal. The challenges posed by natural disasters like tsunamis can be daunting, but they also reveal the strength and determination of individuals and families who refuse to be defeated. Through collaboration, innovation, and education, these communities not only survive but thrive, transforming adversity into a powerful narrative of hope and perseverance. Their stories serve as an inspiration to others facing similar hardships, reminding us all of the importance of community, adaptability, and the relentless pursuit of a brighter future.

Personal Stories of Pre-Tsunami Days

In the quaint coastal village of Kaimana, the days before the tsunami unfolded like a serene painting, vibrant with the colors of daily life. Villagers greeted each other with warm smiles as they went about their routines, whether it was fishing, farming, or gathering at the local market. Children played along the shoreline, their laughter mingling with the gentle sound of waves lapping against the sand. The community thrived on shared traditions and deep-rooted bonds, fostering a sense of security that seemed unshakeable. It was in this idyllic setting that the seeds of resilience were quietly being sown, unbeknownst to the residents.

Maria, a local schoolteacher, often reminisced about the evenings spent telling stories by the beach. The sun would set in a glorious display of oranges and pinks, casting golden reflections on the water. These moments were filled with laughter and the warmth of camaraderie, creating a tapestry of memories that would later inspire the community to come together in the face of disaster. Maria's tales often centered around the strength of the human spirit, a theme that resonated deeply with those who listened. Little did they know, those stories would become a source of hope and courage in the days that followed.

Meanwhile, fishermen like Tomás shared their experiences of the sea, each wave a testament to nature's beauty and unpredictability. His early mornings were filled with the sound of seagulls and the promise of a bountiful catch. Tomás often spoke of the lessons learned from the ocean; respecting its power and understanding its moods were vital for survival. These teachings fostered a deep connection among the fishermen, who relied on each other for both knowledge and companionship. This bond would prove crucial as they faced the impending storm that would forever change their lives.

As the community engaged in various events and festivals, the spirit of togetherness shone brightly. The annual harvest festival was a highlight, where villagers celebrated their hard work with music, dance, and shared meals. This tradition not only honored their agricultural achievements but also reinforced their unity. The laughter and joy during these festivities cultivated a strong sense of belonging, creating a safety net of support that would be invaluable in the aftermath of the tsunami. The villagers unknowingly prepared themselves for the trials ahead through these shared experiences and communal joy.

In those pre-tsunami days, the village of Kaimana thrived as a microcosm of resilience and hope. Each personal story, from Maria's enchanting tales to Tomás's lessons from the sea, contributed to a rich narrative that celebrated life in all its forms. These experiences shaped not just their identities but also their collective strength. As the community faced the tsunami, the essence of their shared history would serve as a beacon of hope, illuminating the path to recovery and survival in the wake of devastation.

Chapter 2: The Day of Destruction

The First Waves

The first waves of the tsunami, a harbinger of chaos, were not just a physical manifestation of nature's fury but also a profound psychological shift for those who experienced them. In coastal communities, the ocean had always been a source of sustenance and serenity, a backdrop for daily life. Yet, on that fateful day, as the first wave broke the tranquility, it transformed into a monstrous force that would reshape lives and landscapes. The initial swell, often underestimated, carried with it the promise of destruction. Residents, caught off-guard, felt a mix of disbelief and dread as they witnessed the water retreating and then surging back with an intensity they had never known.

As the first waves crashed ashore, signals of impending disaster began to ripple through communities. Some individuals, having heard the warnings of previous tsunamis, instinctively understood the danger. They gathered their families, urging them to evacuate to higher ground. Others, however, remained paralyzed by shock, unable to grasp the magnitude of the event unfolding before them. In those critical moments, the instinct to survive clashed with the instinct to stay and protect one's home. The cacophony of sirens, shouts, and the roar of the ocean created a chaotic symphony that would forever echo in their memories.

Survival stories from that day are marked by acts of bravery and quick thinking. Those who witnessed the first wave often recall the surreal beauty of the ocean turning violent. For some, the decision to flee was made in an instant, fueled by a deep-seated understanding that life was worth more than possessions. Families descended from their homes, clutching only what they could carry, driven by a primal instinct to escape the impending doom. Others formed makeshift groups, looking out for one another, proving that even in the face of nature's wrath, the human spirit thrives on connection and solidarity.

In the aftermath of the first waves, the landscape was forever altered, but so too were the lives of those who survived. Communities banded together, sharing resources and stories of courage. The initial devastation gave way to a renewed sense of purpose. Survivors became advocates for preparedness, realizing the importance of education and awareness in preventing future tragedies. They transformed their grief into action, determined to honor those who had lost their lives by ensuring that future generations would be better equipped to face the unknown.

The first waves serve as a reminder of nature's power and the resilience of the human spirit. Through the tales of survival, we learn that while the ocean can be a source of destruction, it is also a catalyst for unity and strength. Each story from that day is a testament to the capacity for hope, healing, and growth in the wake of disaster. As we reflect on the impact of those initial surges, we are inspired to embrace preparedness, fostering communities that can withstand the trials of nature while cherishing the bonds that bring us together amidst adversity.

Eyewitness Accounts of Panic

Eyewitness accounts from those who experienced the tsunami firsthand are powerful narratives that encapsulate the raw emotions and chaos of that fateful day. Survivors often recount the moment they realized something was terribly wrong. The ground shook violently, and the air filled with a deafening roar. Many described a sense of impending doom as they witnessed the ocean receding dramatically, leaving behind a barren seafloor. In those fleeting moments, the realization dawned that the calm sea was about to unleash a catastrophic force. The panic that ensued was palpable, as families scrambled to gather their loved ones, unsure of where to seek safety.

Within the chaos, individual stories emerge that highlight both fear and resilience. One survivor recalls the frantic search for her children amidst the rising tide of panic. The cries of people filled the air, mingling with the sounds of crashing waves and collapsing structures. She vividly remembers the moment she spotted her children, clinging to a tree, and the overwhelming relief that washed over her. This instinct to protect and reunite became a driving force for many, showcasing the depth of human connection even in the face of disaster. Such moments of clarity amid chaos remind us of the strength of familial bonds and the lengths to which people will go to ensure their loved ones' safety.

The aftermath of the tsunami brought a different kind of panic, as survivors struggled to comprehend the devastation around them. The landscape transformed into a scene of utter ruin, with homes reduced to rubble and lives shattered. Eyewitnesses describe the surreal experience of walking through their neighborhoods, searching for familiar landmarks that no longer existed. The sense of loss was overwhelming, yet amidst this despair, stories of hope and courage began to surface. Communities rallied together, offering support and solidarity, proving that even in the darkest times, the human spirit remains unbroken.

Amidst the stories of fear, there are also accounts of remarkable bravery. First responders, often ordinary citizens, became heroes as they rushed into danger to save others. One man, who had been swept away by the waves, recounted how a stranger risked his own life to pull him to safety. These acts of heroism became a beacon of hope for many, illustrating the profound impact of selflessness in times of crisis. Such narratives serve as reminders that even in moments of sheer panic, there can be glimmers of humanity that shine through the darkness.

The collective memory of these eyewitness accounts serves as a powerful tool for education and preparedness. By sharing their experiences, survivors contribute to a growing body of knowledge that emphasizes the importance of community resilience and disaster readiness. Each story is not just a personal tale of survival but also a lesson for future generations on the significance of preparedness, communication, and compassion in the face of natural disasters. Through these accounts, we can learn to confront our fears and emerge stronger, united by the shared experience of overcoming adversity.

The Role of Emergency Services

The role of emergency services in the aftermath of a tsunami is pivotal in ensuring the safety and recovery of affected communities. These dedicated professionals, including firefighters, paramedics, and disaster response teams, work tirelessly to assess damage, provide medical assistance, and facilitate evacuations. Their immediate presence in the wake of such a catastrophic event helps to restore a sense of order and security, allowing individuals to navigate the chaos that often follows a natural disaster. Their training and preparedness are crucial in managing the complexities of disaster response, ultimately saving lives and minimizing further suffering.

Once the tsunami has struck, emergency services are often among the first responders on the scene. They face numerous challenges, including damaged infrastructure, blocked roads, and the threat of aftershocks. Despite these obstacles, their commitment to serving the community shines through. Emergency services carry out search and rescue operations, locating individuals trapped under debris or stranded in isolated areas. Each successful rescue not only reunites families but also reinforces the resilience of communities, highlighting the importance of preparedness and rapid response in mitigating the impact of disasters.

In addition to rescue efforts, emergency services play a vital role in providing medical care to those in need. Hospitals and clinics often become overwhelmed with patients suffering from injuries, trauma, and the effects of exposure. Emergency medical teams are crucial in delivering immediate care, stabilizing patients, and transferring them to facilities equipped to handle their needs. The compassion and expertise displayed by these professionals foster hope and healing in the midst of despair, reminding survivors of the strength found in human connection during the darkest times.

Furthermore, emergency services engage in effective communication with the public, disseminating essential information regarding safety protocols, evacuation routes, and resource availability. Clear and timely updates help to calm fears and reduce confusion among residents. By establishing a reliable flow of information, emergency services empower individuals to make informed decisions about their safety and recovery. This transparency is vital in fostering trust between the community and the responders, ensuring that citizens feel supported and aware of the ongoing efforts to restore normalcy.

In the long-term recovery phase, emergency services continue to be instrumental in rebuilding efforts. They collaborate with local governments, non-profit organizations, and community groups to develop comprehensive recovery plans. Their experience and insight help to shape policies that address vulnerabilities and enhance future disaster resilience. As communities begin to heal, the sustained presence of emergency services serves as a reminder of the collective strength that emerges in the face of adversity, inspiring individuals to come together and work towards a brighter, more prepared future.

Chapter 3: Survival Instincts

The Fight or Flight Response

The fight or flight response is a primal instinct that has been ingrained in human beings for millennia. It is a biological reaction that prepares the body to either confront or flee from perceived threats. In the context of natural disasters, such as tsunamis, this response can mean the difference between life and death. When faced with the sudden onset of a massive wave, individuals are often thrust into a state of heightened awareness and urgency. Their bodies release adrenaline, which increases heart rate, boosts energy supplies, and heightens senses, enabling them to react quickly to the unfolding chaos.

Understanding this response can help survivors better navigate the aftermath of a tsunami. Those who embrace their instinctual reactions may find themselves better equipped to make critical decisions in the face of danger. For some, the urge to fight may manifest as a determination to assist others, whether by helping neighbors evacuate or providing first aid to the injured. Meanwhile, others may feel an intense drive to flee, propelling them towards higher ground. Both reactions, while seemingly opposite, stem from the same survival instinct and highlight the varied ways individuals cope with extreme stress.

The environment in which a disaster unfolds can significantly influence how the fight or flight response is activated. In densely populated coastal areas, the sudden threat of a tsunami can create a chaotic scene filled with confusion and panic. In these situations, clear communication and established evacuation routes become essential. Communities that have prepared in advance—through drills and education—can foster a collective response, allowing individuals to act decisively and effectively. The shared knowledge of what to do when disaster strikes can alleviate some of the fear and uncertainty, empowering people to rely on their instincts while also considering the needs of others.

Moreover, the psychological aftermath of experiencing a tsunami can linger long after the physical dangers have passed. Survivors may grapple with feelings of guilt, anxiety, or post-traumatic stress as they process the chaos and loss. Understanding the fight or flight response is crucial in these moments, as it can provide insight into one's behavior during the disaster. Recognizing that these reactions are natural and rooted in survival can help individuals cultivate self-compassion and seek support from mental health professionals or community resources, facilitating healing and resilience.

Ultimately, the fight or flight response is a testament to the human spirit's resilience in the face of overwhelming adversity. Those who have survived tsunamis and other natural disasters often emerge with profound stories of courage, determination, and community. By sharing these narratives, we not only honor the experiences of survivors but also provide valuable lessons for future generations. Understanding the mechanisms of our instinctual reactions can inspire preparedness and foster a culture of resilience, equipping individuals and communities to navigate the unpredictable tides of nature.

Resourcefulness in Crisis

Resourcefulness in crisis often distinguishes those who merely survive from those who thrive in the aftermath of disaster. In the wake of the tsunami, individuals faced unimaginable challenges, yet many showcased remarkable ingenuity and resilience. The ability to adapt, innovate, and utilize available resources transformed potentially dire situations into opportunities for survival and recovery. These stories highlight the profound strength of the human spirit when confronted with adversity.

One notable example is the story of a small fishing community that lost everything in the tsunami. With their boats destroyed and homes washed away, the residents found themselves at a crossroads. Instead of succumbing to despair, they banded together to salvage what remained. They repurposed debris from their homes to create temporary shelters, using their skills to construct makeshift fishing gear. This resourcefulness not only provided immediate relief but also laid the groundwork for rebuilding their livelihoods. Through collaboration and creativity, they demonstrated that even the most devastating circumstances could be met with a determined spirit.

In another instance, an entrepreneur who lost her shop in the disaster turned her misfortune into an opportunity for community support. Recognizing the lack of access to basic supplies, she mobilized local volunteers to collect donations from neighboring areas. With creativity and perseverance, they set up a temporary market where people could barter goods and services. This not only addressed urgent needs but also fostered a sense of community and mutual aid. Her initiative exemplified how resourcefulness can lead to innovative solutions that benefit the wider population, turning a personal loss into a collective gain.

The role of education and prior knowledge also played a significant part in the resourcefulness exhibited by survivors. Many individuals had training in first aid, construction, or agriculture that became invaluable in the wake of the tsunami. Those who had previously learned skills such as gardening or woodworking found ways to grow food or repair structures using minimal resources. This highlights the importance of preparedness and knowledge as essential tools in navigating crises. Investing in education and skills development can empower communities to respond effectively when faced with natural disasters, enhancing their resilience against future challenges.

Ultimately, the stories of resourcefulness in crisis serve as a powerful reminder of the potential within each individual to rise above circumstances. The human capacity for innovation, collaboration, and adaptation shines brightest in moments of desperation. As these narratives illustrate, the aftermath of a disaster can be a catalyst for growth and transformation. By embracing resourcefulness, communities can not only survive but emerge stronger, paving the way for a more resilient future.

Stories of Immediate Survival

In the aftermath of the tsunami, stories of immediate survival emerged as powerful testaments to human resilience and ingenuity. Individuals faced overwhelming odds, often within moments, and their actions not only preserved their own lives but also the lives of others around them. One such story revolves around a family that was enjoying a quiet evening at home when the disaster struck. As the ground shook violently, the parents instinctively grabbed their children and raced toward higher ground. Their quick thinking and familial bond played a crucial role in their survival, demonstrating the primal instinct to protect loved ones in times of crisis.

Another remarkable tale comes from a group of friends who were visiting a coastal community when the tsunami warning was issued. Instead of succumbing to panic, they quickly devised a plan to reach a nearby hill. Their teamwork was vital; each member took on a specific role, ensuring that everyone was accounted for and moving swiftly. As they ascended, they encountered others who were lost and confused. With compassion and determination, they assisted those in need, showcasing how acts of kindness can flourish even in the direst circumstances. Their story illustrates the importance of community and collaboration during emergencies.

Survival also came from those who found themselves alone in the chaos. A young woman, separated from her family, faced the wave's onslaught with sheer courage. She sought refuge in a sturdy structure, holding her breath as the water surged around her. When the chaos subsided, she emerged disoriented but resolute, determined to reunite with her loved ones. Her journey through the debris-laden landscape was fraught with challenges, yet her unwavering spirit kept her moving forward. This narrative highlights the tenacity of the human spirit, emphasizing that even in solitude, individuals can summon incredible strength to navigate adversity.

The stories of immediate survival often reveal the role of quick decision-making in the face of disaster. A fisherman, caught off guard while working on his boat, had only moments to react when he saw the approaching wave. With instinct guiding him, he abandoned his gear and sprinted toward the shore, taking refuge in a nearby tree. His ability to assess the situation rapidly and act decisively saved his life. This experience underlines the significance of being prepared and aware of one's surroundings, which can make all the difference during natural disasters.

These survival stories are not merely accounts of personal triumph; they serve as lessons for others in the wake of disasters. They remind us of the importance of preparedness, the value of community, and the incredible strength that resides within each individual. As we reflect on these experiences, we recognize that survival is often a collective effort, rooted in compassion and resilience. By sharing these narratives, we not only honor those who endured but also inspire future generations to face their own challenges with courage and hope.

Chapter 4: Finding Shelter

The Search for Safe Ground

In the aftermath of a tsunami, the immediate concern for survivors is finding safe ground. The chaotic scenes unfold as communities are swept into turmoil, and the instinctual drive to seek safety becomes paramount. Those who have experienced such devastating natural disasters often recount their journeys through destruction, highlighting the resilience of the human spirit. The search for safe ground is not just a physical journey but an emotional and psychological one as well, wherein individuals grapple with loss while striving for hope.

Survivors often describe their initial steps post-disaster as a blur, where adrenaline fuels their movements. In those critical moments, the instinct to flee to higher ground becomes a shared understanding among the affected. Families and neighbors band together, navigating through debris and uncertainty, driven by the desire to protect one another. These collective efforts foster a sense of community, where even in the face of despair, individuals find strength in unity. The bonds formed during these harrowing experiences underscore the importance of collaboration in survival.

As survivors reach elevated areas, the reality of their situation begins to set in. The landscape, once familiar and comforting, becomes unrecognizable, and the emotional toll starts to emerge. Stories of survival often reflect a profound transformation, as individuals confront the loss of homes, loved ones, and the life they once knew. Yet, within this grief lies the seed of resilience. Many survivors channel their experiences into advocacy, educating others on preparedness and safety measures, ensuring that the lessons learned from tragedy lead to tangible change.

Resilience is further exemplified through the rebuilding of communities. The search for safe ground is often followed by a collective effort to restore what has been lost. Survivors share their stories of how they contributed to reconstruction, whether through physical labor or by providing support to those in need. This process not only aids in recovery but also serves as a healing mechanism, allowing individuals to reclaim their sense of agency. Through collective rebuilding efforts, communities emerge stronger, fortified by shared experiences and a renewed commitment to safeguard one another.

Ultimately, the search for safe ground transcends the immediate aftermath of a tsunami. It evolves into a journey of healing and empowerment, where survivors transform their experiences into lessons for future generations. The narratives of those who have faced the tide serve as invaluable reminders of the importance of preparedness, community, and resilience. As stories of survival continue to inspire, they reinforce the idea that even in the wake of disaster, the human spirit can prevail, finding safety not only in physical spaces but also in the connections forged through shared adversity.

Community Resilience

Community resilience is a vital component in the aftermath of natural disasters, particularly in the wake of a tsunami. In the face of overwhelming destruction, communities often reveal their strength through unity, collaboration, and shared purpose. This resilience is not merely about recovering physical structures; it encompasses emotional and social rebuilding, fostering a sense of belonging and support among survivors. The stories of those who have faced the turmoil of a tsunami highlight how communities can come together to heal and thrive, transforming adversity into opportunity.

One of the most powerful aspects of community resilience is the ability to mobilize resources effectively. In the aftermath of a tsunami, local organizations, volunteers, and even neighboring towns often rally to provide immediate assistance. This collective effort can lead to the establishment of shelters, food distribution centers, and medical assistance points. These initiatives not only address urgent needs but also create a network of support that reinforces community bonds. Survivors often find strength in helping one another, fostering a spirit of cooperation that can last long after the immediate crisis has passed.

Education plays a critical role in building resilience before and after disasters. Communities that prioritize disaster preparedness training equip their members with the knowledge and skills needed to respond effectively in a crisis. These programs often include workshops on emergency response, first aid, and evacuation procedures. By investing in education, communities can reduce panic and confusion during a disaster, allowing for a more organized and efficient response. Furthermore, as individuals become more knowledgeable, they can share this information, ensuring that the entire community is better prepared for future challenges.

Emotional resilience is equally important in the recovery process. The psychological toll of a tsunami can be profound, with many survivors grappling with loss, trauma, and uncertainty. Communities that prioritize mental health support foster an environment where individuals feel safe to share their experiences and seek help. Support groups, counseling services, and community gatherings create spaces for healing, allowing survivors to connect and process their trauma together. The collective sharing of stories not only validates individual experiences but also reinforces community identity and solidarity.

Finally, the journey of rebuilding often leads to innovation and improvement within communities. As they recover from the devastation, many communities seize the opportunity to reassess their infrastructure and preparedness strategies. This can result in the implementation of more resilient building practices, improved emergency response plans, and enhanced community engagement initiatives. By embracing lessons learned from past experiences, communities not only enhance their resilience but also inspire a sense of hope and determination that resonates with all members. In the face of adversity, the human spirit shines brightly, demonstrating that together, communities can rise against the tide.

Makeshift Shelters and Their Challenges

In the aftermath of a tsunami, the immediate need for shelter becomes a pressing concern for survivors. Makeshift shelters, often thrown together from debris and available materials, can provide a temporary refuge from the elements. These structures, while born out of necessity, reflect the resilience and ingenuity of those affected. The process of creating such shelters often involves utilizing whatever is at hand, whether it be wood from destroyed homes, tarps from emergency kits, or even the remnants of vehicles. In this context, the human spirit shines through adversity, showcasing a remarkable ability to adapt and survive.

However, constructing makeshift shelters comes with its own set of challenges. One of the most significant issues is the lack of stability and safety. Many survivors find themselves in precarious situations, unsure if their shelter will withstand further aftershocks or adverse weather conditions. The anxiety of living in a structure that may collapse at any moment can weigh heavily on the psyche, compounding the trauma already experienced from the disaster. This uncertainty often leads to sleepless nights and a constant state of vigilance, which can hinder the recovery process.

Another critical challenge is the limited availability of resources. In the wake of a tsunami, the landscape can be utterly transformed, leaving survivors to scavenge for materials in a landscape littered with destruction. The competition for usable items can create tension among community members who must rely on each other for support. In some cases, groups may form to share resources and labor, working together to build a stronger communal shelter. This collaboration fosters a sense of solidarity, but it also highlights the disparities in access to materials and skills, as not everyone has the same capacity to contribute.

Moreover, makeshift shelters often lack essential amenities, making daily life incredibly challenging. Survivors may struggle with inadequate protection from the elements, leading to exposure to rain, wind, and cold temperatures. The absence of proper sanitation facilities can result in health hazards, as the risk of disease increases in overcrowded or unsanitary conditions. These challenges can significantly impact the mental and physical health of individuals and families trying to rebuild their lives amidst ongoing difficulties.

Despite these obstacles, the experience of creating makeshift shelters can also foster a sense of community and purpose. As survivors band together, they share not only materials but also stories, skills, and hope. The act of building something, even if temporary, can empower individuals and provide a semblance of normalcy amidst chaos. Ultimately, while the challenges of makeshift shelters are significant, they also serve as a testament to human resilience and the collective effort to forge a path toward recovery in the wake of unimaginable loss.

Chapter 5: The Aftermath

Assessing the Damage

In the aftermath of a tsunami, the landscape is often unrecognizable, transformed into a scene of devastation and chaos. Assessing the damage becomes an essential step not just for recovery but also for understanding the magnitude of the event. Survivors and first responders navigate through debris-strewn streets, where homes once stood and familiar landmarks have vanished. Each step taken reveals stories etched in the ruins—personal belongings scattered, signs of lives once lived, and the overwhelming presence of loss. This process of assessment, though painful, serves as a crucial foundation for rebuilding and healing.

First responders, equipped with training and resilience, play a pivotal role in assessing damage and ensuring safety. They meticulously evaluate structural integrity, identify hazardous materials, and prioritize areas for immediate attention. Their presence provides not just physical assistance but emotional support to those affected. Community members often rally together, sharing information about missing persons and pooling resources. This collaboration fosters a sense of unity, reminding people that they are not alone in their suffering. Together, they can begin to piece together their lives in the face of an overwhelming disaster.

As the days pass, the assessment extends beyond the visible destruction. Emotional and psychological impacts must also be acknowledged and addressed. Survivors grapple with trauma, loss, and uncertainty, which can linger long after the physical damage is repaired. Mental health professionals often join the recovery efforts, providing counseling and support to help individuals process their experiences. Recognizing the emotional toll of a disaster is essential for holistic recovery, ensuring that both physical structures and community spirits can be rebuilt.

The data gathered during damage assessments becomes invaluable for long-term recovery planning. Local governments and organizations analyze this information to prioritize resources and develop strategies for rebuilding. This includes not only infrastructure repair but also enhancing resilience against future disasters. The lessons learned from assessing the damage inform policies that can lead to improved preparedness and response protocols, ultimately reducing vulnerability for communities at risk. By focusing on both current needs and future prevention, communities can emerge stronger from the tragedy.

In the face of such adversity, the act of assessing damage serves as a powerful reminder of human resilience. Each story of survival contributes to a larger narrative of hope and recovery. Communities begin to see beyond the rubble, envisioning a future where they can rebuild not just their homes, but also their lives. The process of assessment, while challenging, becomes a catalyst for transformation, inspiring collective action and a renewed commitment to safety and preparedness. By embracing the lessons learned from the past, communities can forge a path toward a more resilient future, demonstrating that even in the wake of disaster, the human spirit remains unyielding.

Personal Loss and Grief

Personal loss and grief are profound experiences that often accompany the aftermath of natural disasters, such as tsunamis. These events not only disrupt lives physically but also create emotional upheaval that can linger long after the waves have receded. In the wake of such tragedy, individuals face the daunting task of navigating their grief while rebuilding their lives. This journey is unique for each person, shaped by their relationships, experiences, and coping mechanisms. Understanding this process can provide insight into the resilience of the human spirit and the capacity for healing.

The immediate aftermath of a tsunami can be overwhelmingly chaotic, filled with confusion and uncertainty. Survivors may find themselves grappling with the sudden loss of loved ones, homes, and familiar surroundings. This intense emotional pain can manifest in various ways, from shock and disbelief to anger and deep sorrow. It is essential to recognize that these feelings are a natural response to loss, and acknowledging them is the first step toward healing. Communities often come together in the face of such adversity, providing a support network that can help individuals process their grief collectively.

As time progresses, individuals may begin to confront their feelings of loss more directly. This stage often involves reflecting on memories and the impact of their loved ones. Sharing stories about those who have passed can be a powerful tool for healing, allowing survivors to celebrate the lives and legacies of those they lost. Rituals, memorials, and community gatherings can also serve as important avenues for remembrance and connection. These moments not only honor the deceased but also reinforce the bonds among those who share similar experiences of loss.

In the journey of grief, it is crucial for survivors to find healthy coping mechanisms. Engaging in creative expression, such as writing, art, or music, can provide an outlet for emotions that may otherwise feel overwhelming. Additionally, seeking professional support, whether through counseling or support groups, can offer valuable guidance and understanding. The process of grief does not follow a linear path; it ebbs and flows, and individuals must allow themselves to feel and heal at their own pace. Embracing this journey can ultimately lead to personal growth and a renewed appreciation for life.

Ultimately, personal loss and grief teach valuable lessons about resilience and the importance of human connection. While the scars of a tsunami may never fully fade, the strength demonstrated by survivors reveals the capacity to rebuild and find meaning in the aftermath. By sharing their stories and supporting one another, individuals can create a legacy of hope that transcends tragedy. In this way, personal loss becomes not just a source of sorrow, but a catalyst for transformation and a reminder of the enduring power of love and community.

The Struggle for Basic Needs

In the aftermath of a tsunami, the struggle for basic needs becomes an immediate and pressing reality for survivors. As the waters recede, communities are left with devastated infrastructure, disrupted supply chains, and overwhelming emotional trauma. The challenge of securing food, clean water, shelter, and medical care takes center stage, demanding resilience and resourcefulness from those affected. Yet, amidst the chaos, stories of ingenuity and solidarity emerge, showcasing the human spirit's unwavering determination to rebuild and thrive against the odds.

Survivors often find themselves relying on their creativity and community ties to meet their fundamental needs. Makeshift shelters spring up as families gather materials from the debris, utilizing whatever is available to create a safe space. Neighbors come together, pooling resources and skills to establish communal kitchens and water purification systems. These grassroots efforts not only address immediate requirements but also foster a sense of unity and shared purpose, reinforcing social bonds that the disaster threatened to sever. In these moments, the act of survival becomes a collective journey, emphasizing the importance of community in times of crisis.

Access to food presents another critical challenge. In the wake of destruction, agricultural lands may be rendered unusable, and supply routes disrupted, leading to food scarcity. Yet, survivors demonstrate remarkable adaptability, turning to local fishing, foraging, and even cultivating small community gardens in available spaces. Humanitarian organizations often step in, providing essentials and facilitating food distribution networks. The stories of families sharing meals salvaged from the wreckage highlight not only their resourcefulness but also a deep-seated commitment to helping one another, reminding us that compassion can flourish even in dire circumstances.

Clean water becomes a precious commodity, often requiring innovative solutions to overcome contamination from the disaster. Many survivors turn to traditional methods of water purification, while others collaborate with NGOs to implement temporary water filtration systems. The ingenuity displayed in these efforts reflects a broader understanding of sustainability and environmental stewardship. As communities work together to secure this vital resource, they also learn valuable lessons about conservation and the importance of protecting their natural surroundings for future resilience.

Finally, the struggle for basic needs extends to emotional and psychological well-being. The trauma of loss and displacement can weigh heavily on survivors, making access to mental health resources an essential aspect of recovery. Support networks emerge as lifelines, where individuals share their experiences and find solace in one another's company. Local leaders and volunteers often organize counseling sessions and community gatherings, creating safe spaces for healing and rebuilding trust. These initiatives highlight the profound connection between meeting physical needs and addressing emotional scars, reinforcing the idea that survival is not just about enduring but redefining life in the wake of disaster.

Chapter 6: Rebuilding Lives

Community Recovery Efforts

In the aftermath of the tsunami, communities faced the daunting task of rebuilding not just their physical structures but also their social fabric. The devastation reached far beyond the immediate loss of homes and livelihoods; it shattered the sense of security and belonging that had once defined these areas. However, amid the chaos and despair, a remarkable resilience emerged. Local leaders and citizens banded together, drawing on their shared experiences and collective strength to initiate recovery efforts that would lay the groundwork for a brighter future.

One of the most striking aspects of the recovery process was the emphasis on community involvement. Residents who had lost everything found solace in working alongside their neighbors, sharing stories of survival and loss. This communal effort fostered a sense of purpose and solidarity. Community meetings became a platform for discussing needs and priorities, allowing everyone to contribute to the vision of recovery. As these gatherings grew in number, they transformed into forums for hope, where individuals could voice their aspirations and collectively strategize the path forward.

In addition to physical rebuilding, mental health support became a vital component of recovery efforts. Recognizing the psychological toll of the disaster, local organizations and volunteers mobilized to provide counseling and emotional support. Workshops and support groups were established, offering safe spaces for individuals to process their trauma. These initiatives helped to reinforce the idea that recovery was not just about restoring buildings but also about healing hearts and minds. With time, communities began to see the fruits of their labor, as resilience manifested in their ability to cope and thrive despite the scars left by the tsunami.

Moreover, the recovery efforts extended beyond immediate needs to incorporate sustainable practices. Community leaders recognized the importance of building back better, ensuring that the rebuilt infrastructure would be more resilient to future disasters. They sought out innovative solutions, such as elevated housing and improved drainage systems, which not only addressed the vulnerabilities exposed by the tsunami but also empowered residents to take ownership of their environment. This commitment to sustainability resonated deeply with the community, as it symbolized a collective promise to learn from the past and protect their future.

Ultimately, the story of community recovery in the wake of the tsunami is one of hope, resilience, and transformation. The challenges faced were immense, but the unwavering determination of individuals coming together forged new pathways for survival and growth. As these communities rebuilt their homes and lives, they also rekindled the bonds that tied them together, emerging stronger and more united than ever before. Their journey serves as a powerful reminder of the human spirit's capacity to rise against the tide of adversity and create a future filled with promise and possibility.

Personal Stories of Resilience

In the aftermath of a natural disaster, the human spirit often shines brightest, revealing stories of resilience that inspire and uplift. Personal stories of resilience serve as testaments to the strength of individuals who have faced unimaginable challenges. Each account not only highlights the struggles endured but also showcases the unwavering determination to rebuild and move forward. These narratives remind us of our shared humanity and the capacity for hope that exists even in the darkest of times.

One such story comes from a community that found itself at the mercy of the waves during a catastrophic tsunami. Families who lost everything banded together, sharing resources and emotional support. Among them was a woman named Aisha, who, despite losing her home, organized daily meetings to foster a sense of community. Her efforts helped neighbors find solace in shared experiences, turning grief into a collective strength. Aisha's story illustrates how resilience can transform despair into a unified front, empowering individuals to rise above their circumstances.

Another powerful narrative is that of a young boy named Ravi, who was swept away from his family during the disaster. After being rescued, he faced the daunting task of processing his trauma while navigating a new life in a makeshift shelter. With the help of compassionate volunteers, Ravi discovered his passion for art. Through drawing, he expressed his emotions and began to heal. This artistic outlet not only provided him with an escape but also allowed him to connect with others who shared similar experiences, fostering a sense of belonging and hope.

The journey of resilience is often marked by small victories and profound realizations. For instance, a retired teacher named Mr. Kumar lost his entire school to the tsunami. Rather than succumbing to despair, he took it upon himself to rally the community to build a new educational facility. His drive inspired others to contribute time, resources, and expertise. The new school became a symbol of renewal, demonstrating that through collaboration and shared vision, communities can overcome even the most devastating losses.

These personal stories of resilience serve as important reminders of the human capacity to adapt and thrive in the face of adversity. They highlight the power of community, the significance of emotional support, and the importance of finding purpose after loss. As readers reflect on these tales, they are encouraged to recognize their own strength in overcoming challenges, fostering a sense of hope that can transcend difficult circumstances. In the wake of disaster, resilience not only helps individuals heal but also allows communities to emerge stronger, united in their shared experiences and aspirations for a brighter future.

The Role of Volunteers and NGOs

In the aftermath of natural disasters, the role of volunteers and non-governmental organizations (NGOs) becomes paramount in providing immediate relief and long-term recovery. These individuals and groups often step into the breach when government resources are stretched thin or slow to mobilize. Their presence illuminates the resilience of communities, offering hope and practical assistance to those in dire need. Volunteers bring not only their time and skills but also their compassion and determination to help rebuild lives and restore normalcy.

NGOs serve as crucial intermediaries between affected communities and the wider world, effectively channeling resources and expertise to where they are most needed. They often possess the experience and infrastructure necessary to respond quickly and efficiently. By assessing the needs of the disaster-stricken areas, NGOs can coordinate relief efforts, ensuring that food, medical supplies, and shelter reach those who need them most. Their ability to mobilize quickly often saves lives and alleviates suffering during the critical first days and weeks following a disaster.

The impact of volunteers extends beyond immediate relief efforts. They play a vital role in community rebuilding and rehabilitation, providing not just physical assistance but also emotional support. Many survivors find solace in the presence of volunteers, who listen to their stories, share in their grief, and celebrate their resilience. This emotional connection fosters a sense of solidarity, encouraging survivors to engage in the recovery process. The shared experience of overcoming adversity strengthens community bonds and inspires hope for the future.

Training and empowering local volunteers is another significant aspect of the work conducted by NGOs. By equipping individuals with skills in disaster response, first aid, and psychological support, these organizations help create a self-sustaining network of care within affected communities. This capacity-building approach not only enhances local resilience but also prepares communities for future disasters. When individuals are trained to respond effectively, they contribute to a culture of preparedness that can mitigate the impact of future crises.

Ultimately, the collaboration between volunteers and NGOs exemplifies the human spirit's capacity to rise against the tide of adversity. Their collective efforts not only aid in immediate recovery but also lay the groundwork for a more resilient future. As communities heal and rebuild, the contributions of these dedicated individuals serve as a reminder that even in the darkest of times, compassion, solidarity, and a shared commitment to rebuilding can light the way forward.

Chapter 7: Lessons Learned

Preparedness for Future Disasters

Preparedness for future disasters is not merely a reactive measure; it is a proactive approach that can save lives and mitigate the impact of calamities. In the wake of the tsunami, communities learned the importance of early warning systems, which provide crucial time for evacuation and preparation. Investing in technology that can detect seismic activity and trigger alerts can empower individuals to take swift action. This collective awareness transforms a population from passive observers of nature's wrath into active participants in their own safety, cultivating resilience in the face of uncertainty.

Education plays a pivotal role in disaster preparedness. Schools, local organizations, and government agencies must prioritize training programs that equip individuals with the knowledge and skills necessary for survival. Workshops on first aid, emergency response, and survival tactics can foster a culture of readiness. When people understand the potential threats they face and know how to respond, they become more confident and capable in emergencies. This education should extend beyond classrooms to include community drills and simulation exercises, allowing residents to practice their responses in a controlled environment.

Community cohesion is another essential component of disaster preparedness. Building strong social networks ensures that individuals can rely on each other during crises. Communities that foster relationships among neighbors create support systems that can mobilize quickly in times of need. Initiatives that encourage regular meet-ups, collaborative planning, and resource-sharing can enhance collective resilience. When disaster strikes, well-prepared communities can provide immediate aid, share resources, and support those who may be more vulnerable, creating a safety net that is vital for survival.

The significance of personal preparedness cannot be overstated. Individuals and families should develop their own emergency plans, including evacuation routes, communication strategies, and supply kits tailored to their specific needs. Knowing where to go and what to do in a disaster scenario can mean the difference between safety and chaos. Regularly updating these plans and conducting family drills ensures that everyone is familiar with their roles and responsibilities. This personal investment in preparedness empowers individuals to take control of their safety, reducing panic and confusion in the midst of a disaster.

Finally, fostering a culture of preparedness requires ongoing commitment and adaptation. As climate change and urbanization continue to alter the landscape of natural disasters, communities must remain vigilant and responsive. Engaging local governments to assess risks and develop comprehensive disaster response strategies is essential. By learning from past events and investing in future solutions, societies can create a robust framework for disaster preparedness. This continuous evolution not only protects lives but also strengthens the fabric of communities, allowing them to thrive against the tide of uncertainty.

The Importance of Early Warning Systems

Early warning systems play a crucial role in disaster preparedness and response, particularly in the context of natural calamities like tsunamis. These systems are designed to detect potential threats and provide timely alerts to communities at risk. By doing so, they enable individuals and local governments to take swift action, ultimately minimizing casualties and property damage. The implementation of effective early warning systems can mean the difference between life and death, making their importance unmistakable in the wake of devastating events.

The technological advancements in monitoring and communication have significantly enhanced the capabilities of early warning systems. With the integration of satellite imagery, ocean buoys, and seismic sensors, these systems can provide real-time data on seismic activity and ocean conditions. This wealth of information allows scientists to analyze patterns and predict the likelihood of a tsunami following an earthquake. Communities equipped with this knowledge can better prepare for potential evacuations, ensuring that lives are saved when disaster strikes.

Moreover, early warning systems foster a culture of preparedness within communities. When individuals are aware of the potential risks and understand the alerts they receive, they are more likely to take protective actions. Educational initiatives that accompany these systems play a vital role in empowering residents to respond effectively. Regular drills and community meetings can ensure that everyone knows the evacuation routes and safety protocols, reducing panic and confusion during an actual event. This preparedness can build resilience, allowing communities to recover more quickly in the aftermath of a disaster.

The psychological impact of knowing that an early warning system is in place should not be underestimated. The assurance that there are measures to protect against natural disasters can provide a sense of security to residents in high-risk areas. This peace of mind is essential, as it helps to reduce anxiety and fear that can otherwise immobilize communities when faced with the threat of a tsunami. By fostering trust in these systems, communities can stay vigilant and prepared, enhancing their overall resilience.

In conclusion, the importance of early warning systems cannot be overstated. They serve as a lifeline for communities in peril, equipping them with the knowledge and tools necessary to respond effectively to natural disasters. As advancements in technology continue to evolve, it is imperative that we invest in and prioritize the development of these systems. By doing so, we honor the stories of survival that emerge from the wake of calamities like tsunamis and work towards a future where fewer lives are lost, and communities can thrive despite the challenges posed by nature.

Mental Health in the Wake of Trauma

In the aftermath of a traumatic event such as a tsunami, the psychological impact can be profound and long-lasting. Survivors often grapple with a range of emotions, including fear, grief, and confusion. These feelings can manifest in various ways, affecting not only mental well-being but also physical health and daily functioning. Understanding how trauma can influence mental health is crucial for both survivors and those supporting them. Acknowledging these feelings is the first step toward healing, allowing individuals to process their experiences in a safe and constructive manner.

The journey to recovery is often non-linear, with survivors experiencing fluctuations in their emotional state. Some may find themselves reliving the traumatic event through flashbacks or nightmares, while others may develop anxiety or depression. It is essential for survivors to recognize that these reactions are normal responses to abnormal situations. Seeking professional help, whether through counseling or support groups, can provide a vital space for individuals to share their stories, feel understood, and begin to heal. Constructive coping strategies, such as mindfulness and grounding techniques, can also empower survivors to regain a sense of control over their lives.

Community support plays a critical role in mental health recovery after trauma. Survivors often benefit from connecting with others who have faced similar challenges. Community gatherings, peer support networks, and informal meet-ups can foster a sense of belonging and shared experience. By coming together, individuals can exchange coping strategies, celebrate small victories, and collectively process their trauma. This shared resilience not only aids personal recovery but also strengthens community bonds, making it easier to face ongoing challenges together.

Education and awareness about mental health can significantly impact the recovery process. Families and friends of survivors can equip themselves with the knowledge to recognize signs of trauma and offer appropriate support. Encouraging open conversations about mental health can help to destigmatize these issues and create an environment where individuals feel safe to express their feelings. Schools and workplaces can also play a proactive role by implementing mental health resources and training, ensuring that survivors have access to the care they need.

Ultimately, the path to mental health recovery after trauma is marked by resilience and hope. While the scars of a tsunami may remain, they can serve as a reminder of the strength found in survival. As individuals navigate their healing journeys, it is vital to celebrate progress, no matter how small, and to understand that recovery is possible. By fostering a culture of support and understanding, we can ensure that those affected by trauma are not only heard but also empowered to rebuild their lives in the wake of disaster.

Chapter 8: Inspiring Hope

Stories of Triumph Over Adversity

In the wake of a natural disaster, stories of triumph over adversity emerge as beacons of hope, illustrating the resilience of the human spirit. The tsunami that swept through coastal communities not only devastated lives and landscapes but also ignited a fierce determination among those affected to rebuild and recover. These narratives serve as powerful reminders that even in the darkest moments, individuals can rise from the ashes, demonstrating an unwavering commitment to survival and renewal.

One compelling story is that of a small fishing village that experienced catastrophic losses when the tsunami struck. Homes were destroyed, and livelihoods vanished in an instant. Yet, the community came together in a remarkable display of solidarity. Neighbors, once isolated by their individual struggles, united to clear debris, share resources, and support each other emotionally. This collective effort not only expedited recovery but also fostered deeper bonds among villagers, illustrating how adversity can cultivate a profound sense of community.

Another inspiring account comes from a young mother who lost everything in the disaster, including her home and her job. Faced with insurmountable challenges, she refused to succumb to despair. Instead, she sought assistance from local relief organizations and began volunteering her time to help others in similar situations. Through her efforts, she not only found purpose in her own suffering but also inspired those around her to take action. Her story exemplifies how acts of kindness and resilience can transform personal tragedy into a catalyst for communal healing.

Furthermore, there are stories of individuals who turned their passions into pathways for recovery. A talented artist, who had lost her studio to the tsunami, channeled her grief into creating murals that depicted the beauty of her community and the strength of its people. These works of art not only adorned the rebuilt structures but also served as a source of inspiration for others. Her journey illustrates the power of creativity in overcoming hardship, transforming pain into a message of hope and renewal that resonates far beyond the walls of her studio.

Ultimately, the stories of triumph over adversity following the tsunami remind us that while nature can unleash chaos, the human spirit possesses an incredible capacity for resilience. These narratives reflect the strength found in unity, the healing power of compassion, and the ability to transform loss into new beginnings. As communities continue to rebuild, they carry with them the lessons learned from their experiences, forging a future strengthened by the trials they have faced together.

The Power of Human Connection

In the aftermath of a natural disaster, the concept of human connection emerges as a crucial lifeline, transcending the immediate chaos and destruction. Survivors often recount how relationships, whether forged in the midst of calamity or strengthened through shared adversity, provide not only emotional support but also practical assistance. In the wake of the tsunami, communities banded together, sharing resources, shelter, and hope. This collective resilience forms a tapestry of human experience, illustrating how connection can be both a source of strength and a means of recovery.

The stories of individuals who faced the tsunami highlight how profound connections can develop in dire circumstances. Strangers became friends as they navigated the tumultuous waters of grief and loss. An elderly woman, who lost her home, found solace and companionship in a group of volunteers who worked tirelessly to rebuild her community. These relationships, forged in the fires of adversity, often serve as a reminder that while nature can wreak havoc, the human spirit is capable of extraordinary kindness and empathy.

Moreover, the power of human connection fosters a sense of belonging and safety during uncertain times. For many survivors, the emotional turmoil following a disaster can lead to feelings of isolation and despair. However, when individuals come together to share their stories and experiences, they create a supportive environment that encourages healing. Group counseling sessions and community gatherings allowed survivors to express their grief and find solace in shared understanding, reinforcing the notion that they are not alone in their struggles.

In addition to emotional support, human connection plays a vital role in practical recovery efforts. Communities that unite in the face of disaster are often more effective in mobilizing resources and delivering aid. Neighbors sharing tools, knowledge, and manpower can accelerate the rebuilding process significantly. The collaboration between local organizations, government agencies, and citizens exemplifies how collective action can lead to more effective disaster response and recovery, ultimately making communities stronger and more resilient.

Ultimately, the stories emerging from the tsunami's wake underscore the transformative power of human connection. They remind us that in the face of unprecedented challenges, it is our relationships with one another that anchor us and propel us forward. As survivors rebuild their lives, it becomes clear that the bonds formed through shared experiences not only aid in recovery but also inspire hope for a brighter future. The strength found in these connections serves as a testament to the resilience of the human spirit, affirming that together, we can withstand even the most formidable tides.

Looking to the Future

In the aftermath of the tsunami, communities have begun to rebuild not only their physical structures but also their spirits. The resilience demonstrated by those affected serves as a powerful testament to human tenacity. As we look to the future, it becomes clear that the lessons learned from these experiences can lead to stronger, more prepared communities. The stories of survival and recovery are not just tales of loss; they are narratives of hope, illustrating the capacity for individuals and communities to rise from the depths of despair and forge a new path forward.

One of the most significant changes is the emphasis on education and preparedness. Schools and local organizations are now prioritizing disaster preparedness training, ensuring that everyone, from children to adults, understands the importance of readiness. This proactive approach empowers individuals to take charge of their safety, fostering a culture where preparedness is a shared responsibility. Communities are coming together to conduct drills, share resources, and create emergency plans, transforming the fear of future disasters into a collective determination to face challenges head-on.

Furthermore, advancements in technology are reshaping how we respond to natural disasters. Innovations in early warning systems, communication tools, and data analysis have made it easier to predict and respond to events like tsunamis. These technologies not only save lives but also provide a framework for communities to develop robust response strategies. As we harness these tools, we can create a more informed populace that is better equipped to act swiftly and decisively in the face of adversity, ensuring that the lessons of the past are not forgotten but rather integrated into our future planning.

The rebuilding process also presents an opportunity to rethink infrastructure and urban planning. There is a growing movement towards creating resilient cities that can withstand the impacts of natural disasters. By incorporating sustainable practices and disaster-resistant designs, communities are not only enhancing their physical safety but are also fostering a sense of environmental stewardship. This forward-thinking approach encourages a harmonious relationship between people and nature, promoting a future where development does not come at the expense of safety or sustainability.

As we look to the future, the narratives of those who survived the tsunami serve as a guiding light. Their stories remind us that while we cannot control nature, we can control our response to it. Each tale of survival is a call to action, urging us to invest in preparation, embrace innovation, and foster community resilience. By building on the foundations laid by those who came before us, we can create a safer, more connected world that not only endures but thrives in the face of adversity.

Chapter 9: A Call to Action

Advocacy for Disaster Preparedness

Disaster preparedness is a crucial aspect of community resilience, particularly in regions prone to natural calamities like tsunamis. Advocacy for disaster preparedness involves educating individuals and communities about the risks they face, encouraging proactive measures, and fostering a culture of readiness. Communities that prioritize preparedness enhance their ability to respond effectively to disasters, ultimately saving lives and minimizing economic losses. By sharing survival stories and lessons learned, we can inspire action and catalyze change, transforming fear into empowerment.

One of the core components of effective advocacy is raising awareness about the specific threats posed by natural disasters. This includes understanding the signs of an impending tsunami, the importance of early warning systems, and the need for clear evacuation routes. By highlighting real-life experiences of survivors, we can illustrate the impact of preparedness and the difference it can make in critical moments. These narratives serve as powerful reminders that preparedness is not just a personal responsibility but a collective one, requiring the involvement of local governments, organizations, and citizens alike.

Education plays a pivotal role in fostering a culture of preparedness. Workshops, community drills, and informational campaigns can equip individuals with the knowledge and skills necessary to respond to emergencies. Schools can incorporate disaster preparedness into their curricula, teaching children the importance of having emergency plans and knowing how to react in a crisis. Additionally, community leaders can leverage social media and local events to disseminate information, ensuring that preparedness becomes a shared priority. By making education accessible and engaging, we can instill a proactive mindset within communities.

Collaboration among various stakeholders is essential for effective advocacy. Local governments, non-profit organizations, and businesses can work together to create comprehensive disaster response plans. These collaborations can lead to the establishment of resource centers that provide essential supplies and information during emergencies. Furthermore, engaging with local communities in the planning process ensures that the unique needs and concerns of residents are addressed. This inclusive approach not only strengthens community ties but also builds trust among citizens and leaders, fostering a united front in the face of disaster.

Finally, storytelling is a powerful tool in advocacy for disaster preparedness. By sharing survival tales, we can humanize the statistics and highlight the resilience of individuals and communities. These stories not only serve to inform but also to inspire hope and action. When people hear firsthand accounts of survival and recovery, they are more likely to recognize the importance of being prepared. As we compile these narratives in "Against the Tide: Survival Stories from the Tsunami's Wake," we not only honor those who have faced adversity but also motivate others to take the necessary steps toward preparedness, creating a ripple effect of resilience and empowerment across communities.

How Communities Can Prepare

Communities can significantly enhance their resilience against natural disasters like tsunamis by adopting proactive measures that prioritize preparedness and education. One of the most effective strategies is the establishment of comprehensive emergency response plans. These plans should involve local government, emergency services, and community organizations working together to create clear protocols for evacuation, shelter, and communication during a crisis. By conducting regular drills and simulations, communities can ensure that residents are familiar with these procedures, reducing panic and confusion when an actual event occurs.

Education plays a vital role in community preparedness. Schools, local organizations, and community centers can serve as hubs for awareness campaigns, teaching residents about tsunami risks and the importance of emergency kits. Workshops can provide practical skills, such as first aid, basic survival techniques, and how to create a family emergency plan. By fostering a culture of preparedness through education, communities empower individuals to take responsibility for their safety while reinforcing social bonds that are essential during emergencies.

Infrastructure development is another critical component of community preparedness. Local governments should invest in building and maintaining resilient structures, such as sea walls and elevated evacuation routes, that can withstand the impact of tsunamis. Additionally, zoning regulations should be reviewed to prevent new developments in high-risk areas. By prioritizing infrastructure that can mitigate tsunami impacts, communities can protect their residents and reduce potential damage to property and the environment.

Community engagement is essential in cultivating a spirit of preparedness. Residents should be encouraged to participate in local disaster response committees or volunteer organizations dedicated to emergency management. By involving diverse groups in planning and decision-making, communities can ensure that their strategies are inclusive and address the unique needs of all residents, including vulnerable populations. This collaborative approach fosters a sense of ownership and responsibility, motivating individuals to contribute to the overall safety and welfare of their community.

Finally, establishing strong communication networks is vital for effective disaster preparedness. Communities should invest in technologies that facilitate real-time information sharing, such as mobile apps and social media platforms, to keep residents informed during an emergency. Regular updates from local authorities about risks, evacuation routes, and safety measures can significantly enhance community response efforts. By building robust communication channels, communities not only improve their readiness for tsunamis but also strengthen the social fabric that is crucial for recovery in the aftermath of a disaster.

The Role of Education in Survival

Education plays a pivotal role in shaping the responses of individuals and communities in the face of natural disasters, particularly in the aftermath of catastrophic events like tsunamis. Knowledge equips people with the tools they need to prepare for emergencies, understand the risks associated with their environment, and develop effective survival strategies. In regions prone to tsunamis, educational initiatives focusing on disaster preparedness can significantly enhance the resilience of communities, ultimately reducing loss of life and property.

Schools and community organizations serve as vital platforms for disseminating information about disaster preparedness. Through structured programs, residents learn about evacuation routes, emergency kits, and the importance of early warning systems. Such education fosters a culture of preparedness, where individuals are not only aware of the dangers but also actively engaged in their own safety and that of their neighbors. This proactive approach can save lives by ensuring that people know what to do when disaster strikes, minimizing panic and confusion.

Moreover, education extends beyond mere survival tactics; it encourages a deeper understanding of the science behind natural phenomena. By teaching students and community members about how tsunamis are generated and the geological factors at play, individuals can better appreciate the importance of following safety protocols. This knowledge not only empowers them to act more decisively during emergencies but also instills a sense of responsibility for advocating safety measures within their communities, creating a ripple effect of awareness.

In the aftermath of a tsunami, educational programs can also aid in recovery efforts. Communities that have prioritized education are often more adept at rebuilding and adapting to new challenges. Training in skills such as emergency response, first aid, and mental health support can transform survivors into effective responders, fostering resilience and solidarity. As they share their knowledge and experiences, individuals contribute to a collective memory that informs future generations, ensuring that lessons learned are not forgotten.

Ultimately, education is a vital tool in the survival toolkit of any community facing the threat of natural disasters. It cultivates awareness, preparedness, and resilience, enabling individuals to navigate the complexities of a post-disaster landscape. By investing in educational initiatives, societies can reinforce their capacity to withstand and recover from the impacts of tsunamis, transforming vulnerability into strength and creating a legacy of survival that extends far beyond the immediate crisis.

Chapter 10: Reflections on Survival

Personal Growth Through Adversity

Personal growth through adversity is a powerful theme that resonates deeply in the wake of catastrophic events, such as tsunamis. In the aftermath of such disasters, individuals often find themselves faced with not only physical destruction but also emotional and psychological challenges that can lead to profound personal transformation. The experience of surviving a tsunami can serve as a catalyst for change, pushing individuals to reevaluate their priorities, relationships, and their own capabilities. This journey through adversity often reveals the strength of the human spirit and the potential for resilience that lies within us all.

Survivors of tsunamis frequently report a newfound appreciation for life following their experiences. The sheer unpredictability of nature reminds us of the fragility of existence, prompting many to embrace their lives with renewed vigor. For some, this means pursuing long-held dreams that were previously sidelined by the routine of daily life. The realization that life is fleeting can inspire individuals to take bold steps toward their goals, whether that involves starting a new career, cultivating meaningful relationships, or engaging in community service. Each story of survival is unique but often echoes a common thread: the drive to live life to its fullest after facing the unimaginable.

Moreover, navigating the aftermath of a tsunami fosters a sense of community and interdependence among survivors. In times of crisis, people often come together in ways they never envisioned. This collective experience can lead to stronger bonds and a greater sense of belonging. Individuals learn to rely on one another for support, sharing their stories and coping mechanisms. The connections formed in the face of adversity can become lifelong relationships, enriching the lives of those involved. Through shared experiences, survivors cultivate empathy and understanding, allowing them to grow not only as individuals but also as a cohesive community.

The challenges posed by a tsunami also provide fertile ground for developing problem-solving skills and adaptability. Survivors are thrust into situations where quick thinking and resourcefulness become vital. The ability to assess a situation, devise a plan, and implement it effectively can lead to increased self-confidence and a sense of empowerment. Many find that they possess far greater resilience than they ever thought possible. This newfound skill set is not limited to disaster scenarios; it often translates into everyday life, enabling individuals to tackle personal and professional challenges with a newfound perspective and determination.

Ultimately, personal growth through adversity is a testament to the human capacity for change and renewal. The stories of those affected by tsunamis are filled with instances of individuals rising from the depths of despair to create new paths forward. Each narrative serves as a reminder that even in the darkest moments, there is potential for light. The lessons learned from adversity can inspire others to embrace their own challenges, fostering a cycle of growth that transcends individual experiences. Through the lens of survival, we discover that adversity can be a powerful teacher, guiding us toward a deeper understanding of ourselves and our place in the world.

The Lasting Impact of Survival Stories

Survival stories from natural disasters resonate deeply within us, often serving as profound reminders of human resilience and the enduring spirit of survival. In the aftermath of a catastrophe like a tsunami, the narratives that emerge not only document individual experiences but also weave a larger tapestry of hope and endurance. These stories allow us to connect with the raw emotions of those affected, fostering empathy and understanding. They remind us that amidst chaos, there are tales of courage, quick thinking, and the unyielding will to survive, which can inspire and motivate others who face their own challenges.

The impact of these survival stories extends beyond individual experiences; they play a crucial role in shaping community responses to disasters. When survivors share their tales, they often highlight the importance of preparedness, resilience, and communal support. These accounts provide valuable lessons that can inform how communities respond to future crises. By learning from the experiences of others, communities can build stronger support systems, develop effective emergency plans, and cultivate a culture of preparedness that can save lives in the face of adversity.

In addition to their immediate community impact, these narratives contribute significantly to the broader discourse on disaster management and recovery. They often serve as case studies for researchers and policymakers, illustrating the complexities of human behavior during crises. The insights gained from these stories can lead to improved response strategies, better resource allocation, and enhanced training for first responders. As a result, the lasting impact of survival tales can be seen in the development of more robust frameworks for disaster preparedness and recovery, ultimately reducing vulnerability in the face of future disasters.

Moreover, survival stories can have a profound psychological effect on both survivors and those who hear their accounts. For survivors, sharing their experiences can be a cathartic process, helping them to make sense of their trauma and begin the healing journey. For those outside the experience, these tales can foster a sense of solidarity and a deeper appreciation for the fragility of life. They can also motivate individuals to take proactive steps in their own lives, whether that means preparing for potential disasters or cultivating a greater sense of gratitude for their own circumstances.

Ultimately, the lasting impact of survival stories lies in their ability to inspire action and foster a sense of community. They remind us that in the face of overwhelming odds, humans have an incredible capacity to adapt, overcome, and support one another. By sharing these powerful narratives, we not only honor the resilience of those who have faced disaster but also empower future generations to confront their own challenges with courage and determination. The stories of survival are not just tales of individual triumph; they are essential threads in the fabric of human experience, showcasing our collective strength and the unbreakable bonds that emerge in times of crisis.

Embracing Life After Loss

Embracing life after loss is a journey that requires resilience, courage, and an unwavering spirit. For those who have endured the heart-wrenching aftermath of a natural disaster, the path forward can often feel overwhelming. However, within the depths of despair, there exists an opportunity for growth and renewal. This chapter explores the transformative power of embracing life after loss, highlighting the importance of hope, community, and personal reflection in the healing process.

In the wake of a tsunami or similar catastrophe, individuals face not only physical destruction but also emotional upheaval. The initial phase of recovery often involves grappling with grief and shock. It is vital to acknowledge these feelings rather than suppress them. Allowing oneself to grieve is a crucial step in the healing journey. By honoring the lost and recognizing the pain, survivors can begin to process their experiences, paving the way for eventual acceptance and peace. This phase can be challenging, but it is also a necessary part of moving forward.

Community plays a pivotal role in the recovery process. In times of tragedy, people often find strength in unity, as they band together to support one another. Engaging with others who have shared similar experiences can foster a sense of belonging and understanding. Support groups, local organizations, and even informal gatherings can provide a safe space for individuals to share their stories, express their feelings, and rebuild connections. These relationships can serve as a lifeline, reminding survivors that they are not alone in their struggle and that together, they can rise from the ashes.

As survivors begin to rebuild their lives, they often discover new passions and purposes that drive them forward. This stage of embracing life after loss can be marked by a renewed commitment to personal growth and community involvement. Many individuals find solace in volunteering, whether it be through helping others in need or participating in local rebuilding efforts. This act of giving not only aids in the recovery of the community but also fosters a sense of fulfillment and hope within the individual, transforming pain into purpose.

Ultimately, embracing life after loss is about finding meaning in the midst of chaos. Each story of survival is unique, yet there are common threads that bind these narratives together. Resilience, connection, and a desire to rebuild serve as powerful reminders that even in the darkest moments, there is light to be found. By embracing life with courage and determination, survivors can honor their past while forging a path toward a brighter future, proving that hope can flourish even in the wake of devastation.

Vivamus vestibulum ntulla nec ante.

Lorem ipsum dolor sit amet, consectetur adipiscing elit, sed do eiusmod tempor incididunt ut labore et dolore magna aliqua. Ut enim ad minim veniam, quis nostrud exercitationullamco laboris nisi ut aliquip ex ea commodo consequat. Duis aute irure dolor in reprehenderit involuptate velit esse cillum dolore eu fugiat nulla pariatur. Excepteur sint occaecat cupidatat nonproident, sunt in culpa qui officia deserunt mollit anim id est laborum.

www.ingramcontent.com/pod-product-compliance
Lightning Source LLC
Chambersburg PA
CBHW040235240726
48664CB00001B/135